Cover art by Ian M. Ryan

Stargazing

Ian M. Ryan

ISBN: 9798345784419

DEDICATION

I'd like to dedicate this book to Mrs. Schanz, my high school English teacher. Without you, none of this would be possible. The faith that you had in me to write and the confidence you had in me is something I'll never forget, and I'll never take for granted. You allowed me to "Stargaze" at the idea of being an author, and you pushed me to actually achieve it. This one is for you!

CONTENTS

READ OTHER TITLES BY IAN M. RYAN

Written and Published by Ian M. Ryan:
Love in the Lilacs and Other Science Fiction Shorts

Written in the Stars

Stargazing

Included in Anthologies:
Beyond the Levee and Other Ghostly Tales – Peter Talley

Institutionalized: 9/24 Down in the Dirt, v223 – Scars Publications

ACKNOWLEDGMENTS

Renee (RJ) Walker is a talented artist from Bremen High School in Illinois. We crossed paths at an event that I was speaking at. Her artwork is amazing, and you should check it out on her Instagram page, @rjplaysanime. See her art on page 33.

One of my photographers is (at the time of release) my fiancé, Abby, who supports me always and contributed to this book in ways that she didn't know she was. See her photograph on page 26.

Molly Ryan, my sister and best friend, is included in this book as a photographer. She has some pretty amazing talent, and you can see her photos on pages

I'd like to also acknowledge God for giving me my purpose of writing and spreading the truth about mental health issues. If you need help, you can come to me, and I will help you get that help. The world is a better place with you here.

Free Mental Health Outlets

- Suicide Prevention Assistance - Call/Text 988 for
- Mental Health Hotline - 866-903-3787
- Crisis Text Line - *Text HOME to* 741741
- Mental Health Apps for Phones (Calm, MindShift, etc…)

HAUNTED

I am but a man,

Engaged by the present,

Haunted by the past,

And moments of resent.

Putting my head down,

Slowly moving forward,

The life I wanted,

No longer one I can afford.

The echoes of the past,

Refusing to resign,

Haunting me,

Every second of time.

PILLS

I'll just take one or two,

I swear that'll do.

But one or two,

Turns to three or four,

Then that leads

To so much more.

The pain was never physical,

It was all mental,

Pills were the only way,

I could get some relief.

I'm never enough

And life has been rough...

So, I take more

No, I *need* more.

I want to be numb,

I don’t want to feel a thing.

So, I take more pills,

And wait for the chills,

For the quiet in my mind,

Emotions going blind.

And for a while I’m okay,

Until the effects wear away.

And I’m left with the man in the mirror,

Wishing I could see him clearer,

Not just an outline,

Where a good man used to reside.

So, I take more pills,

As my mind runs for the hills,

Away from my depression,

The pills becoming a therapy session.

But these pills are not my friends
They're the opposite,

They bring me more pain,
And they hurt my brain,

But I take them anyway,
Because I am their prey.

BURN BRIGHT

We burn bright

Flaming along our route.

As we bump and collide,

Getting thrown about.

Searching the world

Always discerning.

While our flame merely lit,

The Earth keeps turning.

Burn Bright

For the world to see you,

Because just like the stars,

We all will burn out, too.

2AM THOUGHTS

2am on a Friday,

Playing video games with my best friend,

Never did I dream,

That these days would end.

Past midnight,

Overloaded on caffeine,

That's what you do,

When you're 15.

2am on a Friday,

Busy kissing her.

No care in the world,

Of how mad your parents were.

That's what life was,

Reckless and free,

Not worried about tomorrow,

When you're 17.

2am on a Friday, at the bar legally,

Drinking a little too much,

To have fun or to hide the pain?

To be happy, or use it as a crutch?

We all have things,

To help mask how we feel,

Because when you're 21,

Life gets real.

2am here,

Thinking of the past,

I never listened,

When they said it moved too fast.

Working too much,

Paying far too many bills,

At 25,

Figuring out what fulfills.

One thing I know,
No matter how old you get,

You will look back,
And the past will give you a fit.

30 is jealous of 21,
50 is jealous of 30.

People are jealous of the young,
Caught up in what could be.

ENJOY THE RIDE

I hate you for making me think I wasn't good enough,

And I hate you for making everything such a big deal.

I hate you for not getting the help that you needed,

And I hate you for who you became because of how you'd feel.

I hate you for losing focus on the good,

And I hate you that were so focused on the bad.

I hate you for telling yourself you hated you,

And I hate that a girl drove you mad.

I hate you for focusing so much on a sport,

I hate you for not realizing your other passions sooner.

I hate you for what you did to your body,

And I hate that you showed your pain through humor.

I hate that you didn't tell people the truth,

I hate that you didn't stand up for yourself.

I hate that you tried to overdose,

I hate that you didn't leave the pills on the shelf.

I hate that you have diabetes,

I hate that you didn't talk in the therapy sessions,

I hate that you have anxiety,

I hate that you have depression,

But mostly,

I hate that you hated you.

Despite all of this hate,

I'm proud of you.

I'm proud that you made it through,

I'm proud that you're still here today.

I'm proud that you let love in,

I'm proud to say that you've grown,

I'm proud that you let others in,

I'm proud you didn't do this on your own.

I'm proud of you for reading the Bible,

I'm proud that you found God again,

I'm proud that you talked to a therapist,

I'm proud that you're better than you've ever been.

I'm proud you found new hobbies,

I'm proud that you travel,

I'm proud you're on top of your mental health,

I'm proud you don't let your episodes unravel.

I'm proud of the way you live life now,

I'm proud to say that you were me.

This is just a letter,

Reminding you of your past.

Reminding you that the good times,

Come back around and will last.

Life is a roller coaster of bad and good,

And at times they will collide.

So, stop worrying about what could go wrong,

And just...

Enjoy the ride.

THE HARDEST THING (A LYRICAL POEM)

When I was leavin

Leavin you,

I couldn't help thinkin,

Of all that we could do.

I meant it when I said

I love you,

As I was leavin,

That's the hardest thing to do.

When you took your final breath,

I couldn't help but cry.

It's not fair

When a loved one dies.

Because now life's full,

Of memories of you.

And sayin goodbye,

That was the hardest thing to do.

I feel you in the wind,

I see you in my dreams.

But life isn't always fair,

And that's how it seems.

Because it'll leave you broken,

In so much pain.

It'll leave you worn down,

Under a cloud of rain.

But getting up,

Knowing you'll get through.

Trust me it's worth it,

Even if that's the hardest thing to do.

GROWN UP

Babies crying,

Products we're always buying,

Doorbells constantly ringing,

And I ain't lying,

My bank account,

It's never been lower.

Often, I wish time,

Would move a little slower.

This is life,

As a grown up.

Used to hate coffee,

Now I drink it every day.

I gotta watch my mouth now,

Back then I didn't care what I'd say.

I'm a believer of "money should grow on trees",

And now I'm counting calories,

Because I'm squeezing into jeans,

They didn't teach me of days like these.

This is life,

As a grown up.

I have bills,

For things I didn't know I even bought.

"I'd like to be a kid again",

Is now my favorite thought.

But I take all my meds,

I put on a smile,

And I show everyone,

It's worth every trial,

Because this is life,

As a grown up.

STARGAZING

I’ve always been a fan,

Of looking at the sky.

Seeing the moon,

Gazing at the stars,

They all looked so free,

As they’d fly by you and me.

I was amazed,

By the sheer beauty.

Like the first time,

I caught a glimpse of you.

Looking into your eyes,

Seeing them look back at me.

For the first time,

This man was truly seen.

I finally knew what it meant,

I was stargazing.

But not at the moon,

Not at the stars,

No, this time,

It was at who you are.

The sparkle,

The shine,

I have been stargazing,

Since the first time your eyes met mine.

Aurora Borealis - Abby Markowski

WHISKEY INTO WINE

She saved my life,

Wasn't even what I was looking for.

But now I don't remember,

The man I was before.

Pills to chase a memory,

Drinking drowns the pain.

She saved me from myself,

The devilish thoughts in my brain.

She took the whiskey,

And turned it into wine,

When she became mine,

God showed me a work so divine.

Now my whiskey glass,

Is back on the shelf.

I'm getting better day-by-day,
No longer heading astray.

Life was dragging me down,
Doing the wrong things,

Now I see the joy,
In my life that no drug brings.

You saved this man,
When you became mine.

You took my whiskey,
And turned it into wine.

FOOTPRINTS

They're on the moon,

They're on the beach,

Sunken in the mud,

Somehow all in reach.

They get washed away,

Only seen by a few.

My life changed,

By the footprints of you.

I'm a happier guy,

And a stronger man,

Meeting you,

Is when my life began.

STRENGTH

I won't be dragged down by what they say,

Time is too precious to give away.

I am stronger than my depression of today,

Because of the prospect of tomorrow.

I will not lose my way,

I will not live today in sorrow.

THE POET

Poetry is different,

For everyone who writes it.

Sometimes poems rhyme,

Some use humorous wit.

Some poems are about love,

Some are about hate,

Some poems are bad,

Some are great.

Poets would agree though,

About one thing,

That poetry,

Can be what people need.

It's an outlet,

For what's in our hearts and our minds,

Speaking about everything,

We hold deeply inside.

Poetry opens your mind,

While it opens our hearts,

Poetry really is,

A unique work of art.

It isn't perfect,

It really is quite hard,

But this can be healing,

For times when you were scarred.

Yes, I am a poet,

I know I'm not the best,

But my poetry has meaning,

And it allows my mind to rest.

If someone feels a bit better mentally,

After reading my poetry,

That would be my dream,

That would truly fulfill me.

The Poet – RJ Walker

DREAM

Last night,

I had a dream,

I met up,

With the younger me.

We talked,

We laughed,

Both shocked,

At how the time passed.

I was now chubby,

He described me as "old."

He was energetic

And overly **BOLD**...

It was crazy,

How I used to be.

I was feeling lost,

This is what I needed to see.

Someone so into life,

And his future,

How would he react

When I told him I was a loser?

I told him about grief,

I told him of loss,

We talked about broken dreams,

How life doesn't show remorse.

We talked about injuries,

And the friends we made,

The friends we lost,

And the girls we date.

The hearts we broke,

The ones who broke ours,

And the ones we think about,

For hours and hours.

As his tears fell,

Like when rain would pour,

"So, we *didn't* get our dreams?"

"No... we got way more..."

We found love,

We found a career,

It isn't what we expected,

But we love it here.

Your best friend,

She had a daughter,

And you became,

The Godfather.

Life isn't easy

But I promise it's worth it.

It's not what you'll imagine

But you'll love it more than you admit

Your younger self smiles

And it truly beams.

In that moment he realized

You got more than you ever dreamed.

GHOSTS

When I'm anxious,

When I'm depressed,

I see ghosts,

I see them all the time.

I see who I used to be,

I see the happy kid,

The one with no worries in the world,

The one who didn't have bills to pay.

I see my parents not having to worry,

About finding their son at home,

Not alive because he was too depressed,

Or in the bathroom bleeding again.

My sister,

Not having to worry about her little brother overdosing.

His brothers,

Not having to call him in a hospital asking if he's getting better.

They may not be the ones from the movies,

But you're darn right I see ghosts.

INTO THE MIND OF THE AUTHOR

For a long time, I was searching for my purpose on this Earth. I was confused with so many things that happened to me and my family as I was growing up, that at times it felt like I didn't have one. God led me to baseball, and I would put my heart, soul, and all of my time into it. Eventually, baseball was no longer part of my life full-time. College came to an end, and I wasn't playing every day anymore, I wasn't practicing, and I honestly had lost my love for the game that my life revolved around for over 18 years.

Mentally, this broke me down. How could I lose the one thing that kept me going for so long? Was I losing myself because I lost this sport? I'm not sure if this is a common thought in people, but for me, it was common whenever anything changed. When I would have a relationship end, it was the end of the world. When I had family pass away, it was the end of the world. When anything was different, it was the end of the world. I realized that change was my enemy. Change was what drove my anxiety. Change was the one thing I had no control over, and that terrified me. I hated change, but I witnessed it every... single... day.

During this time of figuring out what my next/forever purpose would be, I fell into writing. That's what this first part of Stargazing is truly about. Feeling down about life, falling into addiction, realizing you're making some really bad decisions, falling into people and things that you need, and ending up in a better place than you ever could have imagined. This change though, couldn't happen without the support group I built to help me with my mental health.

MIRROR, MIRROR

I looked in the mirror,

I didn't see me.

I hated who I saw,

But how could this be?

Sometimes the person in the mirror,

Is an image made in our mind.

And not the reflection

Of the true person inside.

AWAKE

I've been up for a while now.

Haven't been able to sleep.

I'm not okay,

But what the hell is wrong with me?

I can't relax my mind,

I'm at war in my head,

While the rest of the world,

Is asleep in their beds.

I can't pinpoint a reason,

That I'm like this.

Why every little, tiny thing,

Turns into a life crisis...

I'm anxious,

I'm stressed,

I'm annoyed,

I'm depressed.

This world is beating me down,

I can't win.

I can't sleep,

Because of this battle I'm in.

But still, I close my eyes,

Not to go to sleep,

I'm trying to forget,

Everything that cuts me so deep.

That's what keeps me up.

Each and every mistake.

The burden that I am,

Keeping me awake.

SNOW

Like snow,

We shall fall.

Whether on bare cement,

Or on top of padding,

The fall makes us stronger,

And we land at our new destination.

Making a new path for ourselves,

Until our time is up and we are sent packing.

But again,

Just like snow,

We're absorbed into our cloud,

Until we shall fall again.

And the cycle repeats,

We make a new way,

Full steam ahead.

Until our full shape is built one day.

Snow - Molly Ryan

SOMEONE LIKE YOU

Looking at the stars,

I think of you.

Used to watch together,

Baffled by the view.

On the trampoline,

Or sitting in the driveway.

In the middle of the night,

I'd always wanna stay.

Living in different cities,

Went to different schools.

We always made it work,

Loving like fools.

Now I look at the same stars,

Wondering how I got this far.

We aren't together,

And that left a permanent scar.

It's not about the stars,

It's about me.

Getting caught up,

In all that we could be.

But you're long gone,

Found a new life now.

Everyone tells me to move on,

But how?

How do I forget the best times,

How do I forget that smile?

How do I forget about,

A love so versatile?

One that was loyal and fair,

One that was true.

How do I forget,

Someone like you?

BURDEN

And in that moment,

I knew him as he knew me,

Just a burden

to everyone he'd meet.

As I imagined my life,

I didn't see anything as good...

Maybe I saw myself,

As misunderstood?

Lost was this man,

Just trying to be happy.

But that happy man was gone,

No smile left to see.

With every step

And every breath,

Were there any good thoughts?

No, all he thought of was death.

Because all that he was,

Was just a burden to the rest,

These were my thoughts,

When I was depressed.

LIFE IS A DREAM

They say this life is a dream,

But if that's true,

I don't wanna wake up,

Unless I'm next to you.

I was scared of the future,

Stuck living in the past,

But since I met you,

I finally want this life to last.

Your laugh,

Your eyes,

Meeting mine at the right time,

Even if you were a surprise.

I never saw you coming,

When you wandered into me,

But of all the surprises I've gotten,

You are by far the best thing.

So, if I'm just dreaming,

Won't you let me sleep,

Because for once,

This is a life I want to keep.

WORLD IN MY ARMS

Not sure how I got here,

With you next to me.

The best thing in my life,

I don't know what you see.

I'm a man that's been broken,

Hurt a time or two.

But something about this is different,

I'm just drawn to you.

You see ***me,***

Like no one else could,

And you let me be me,

Like I always should.

I don't have to hide,

My emotions or my feelings,

And when I'm inside hurting,

You start my healing.

I don't know how I got here,

You laying your head on my chest.

Listening to you breathing,

As you start to rest.

The tv is on,

Watching some football game,

But now I'm in my head,

Wondering how all this became.

We were strangers,

Just a few months ago,

Now I'm holding on tight,

Not wanting to let go.

I'm holding the world in my arms,

As she sleeps away the night,

And for the first time in my life,

I know I finally got it right.

KISSES THROUGH THE WINDOW

Blowing kisses through the window,

Waving before I drive down the road,

Wishing I didn't have to leave you,

But knowing one day you will be my home.

COUNTRY MUSIC

I've always loved music,

And I was raised on country.

But the way I see it,

Country sort of raised me.

Tim McGraw taught me a lot,

To give people a reason for rememberin',

When he wrote that he saw God that day,

George Strait taught me to let God in.

Mitch Rossell,

Penned Son, Hollywood, and Ran into You.

He taught me to write with passion.

And I love his cover of Run, too.

Kacey taught me to follow my arrow,

Shania taught me what it'll be like when I meet the one.

Faith taught me how to love a woman.

Dolly made 9 to 5 fun.

Urban taught me about wanting to love someone.

Church taught me he was a sinner like me,

Paisley got me to love camouflage,

Bentley told me how important my last name would be.

Taylor Swift taught me it was okay to change,

Trisha taught me even Tommy could win.

Carrie made me want to have an "All-American" daughter.

Sara Evans taught me I get stronger when I beat the pain within.

Some of the names are now different,

But I listen to country music still,

Because I love country music,

And I always will.

BEAT UP STREET

A gallon-sized glass jar

Full of money.

When you'd shake it

It'd sound real funny.

It wasn't much.

Behind the door of my parents' closet.

We didn't have it all,

But we'd have what we'd need.

Living in a house

On that beat up street.

Four older siblings,

Looking out for me.

There was so much love,

That I could see.

All in the same house

With little space

No wonder our rooms

Were all a “disgrace.”

We didn’t have much,

But we’d have what we’d need.

Living in a house,

On that beat up street.

It’s just Tommy and me,

Living with my parents now

Sometimes I look back

And think wow...

How'd we get here?

I wish I'd known,

My whole world

Would be on their own.

We didn't have much,

But we'd have what we'd need.

Living in a house,

On that beat up street.

So many good times,

I hold them all with me

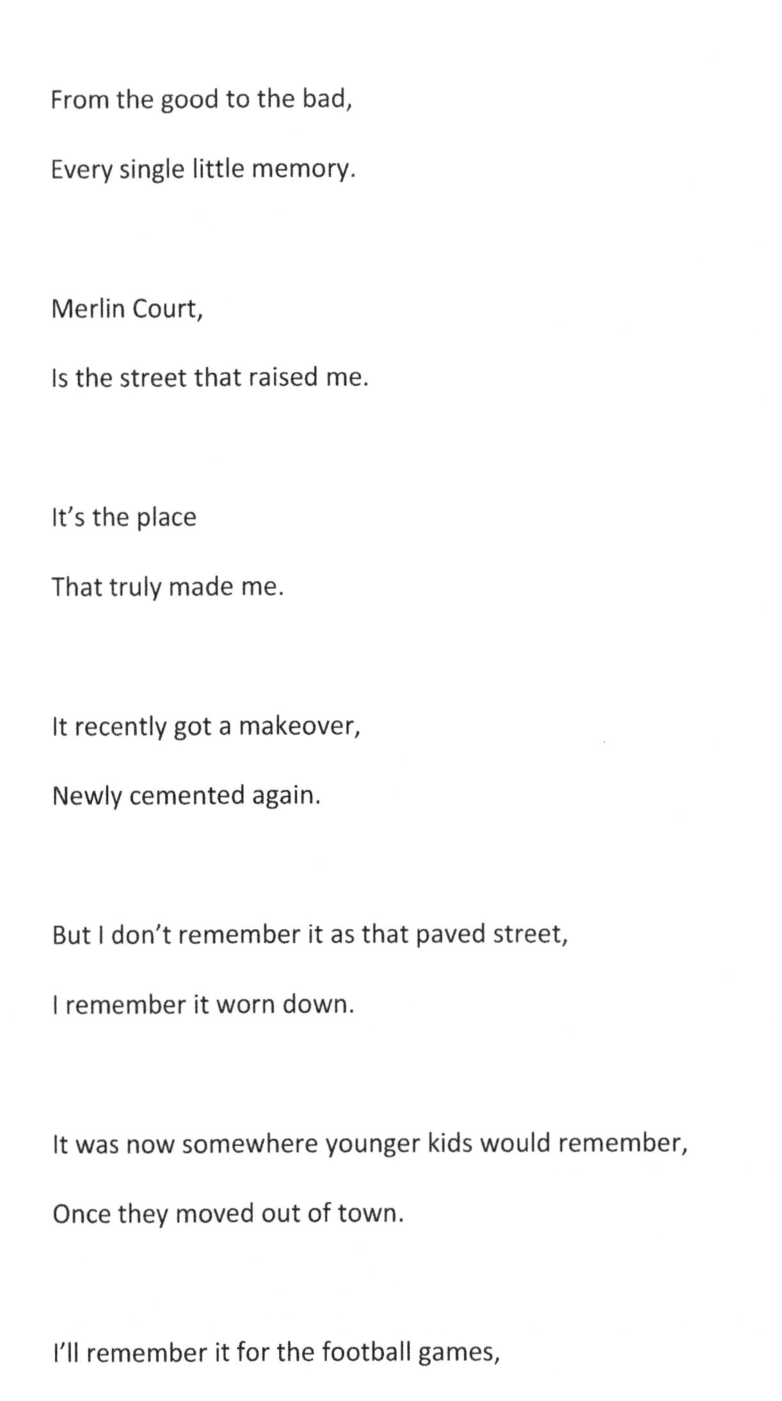

From the good to the bad,

Every single little memory.

Merlin Court,

Is the street that raised me.

It's the place

That truly made me.

It recently got a makeover,

Newly cemented again.

But I don't remember it as that paved street,

I remember it worn down.

It was now somewhere younger kids would remember,

Once they moved out of town.

I'll remember it for the football games,

And learning how to drive.

Taking my telescope out for the first time,

And where I felt the most alive.

We didn't have much

But we'd have what we'd need.

Living in a house

On that beat up street.

Home – Molly Ryan

GREW UP LIKE THAT

I grew up next to my best friends,

Hanging out past when the moon came out.

Juice boxes in the fridge,

And a snack drawer rustled about.

We didn't have a curfew,

But knew when late, was too late.

If we were past that time,

We knew our fate.

I wish that everybody,

Grew up like that.

I knew a love,

That only a mother could show.

I had a dad,

Who helped me grow.

They got me through,

When the times were tough.

I'll never tell them,

I love them enough.

I wish that everybody,

Grew up like that.

I always had a ride,

And food on my plate.

If we hadn't prayed,

We knew we had to wait.

My older siblings,

Helped me along the way.

Like when I was mad,

They taught me what to say.

I wish that everybody,

Grew up like that.

I grew up in a small town,

Where everybody waved.

We stopped during our walks,

Just to say hey.

You'd wish them well,

They'd do the same.

Because being kind to each other,

Was just what you'd do.

And if one person was mad at you,

Everyone knew.

I wish that everybody,

Grew up like that.

Now that I'm older,

And I'm coming back to town,

The faces have changed,

buildings moved around.

One thing stayed true,

The love I have for thee,

This town and the people that raised me.

Now I wish and pray,

That everybody,

grew up like that.

PEOPLE ARE STARS

So many different colors,

So many different shades,

The world moves on,

Even when one fades.

There is no question,

We are not the same,

We are called "stars,"

When we rise up to fame.

We belong to constellations,

Some big, and some small.

Some prefer to be alone,

"Rogue" you might call.

Sometimes they burn out,

Others brightly shine,

Some stay consistent,

Which is normal,

Which is fine.

Yet,

We all have something that sets us apart,

Like the shine of the Northern Star.

Someone who guides us home,

You know who they are.

We all have our own marks,

What makes us who we are.

Things that others see,

Both near, and far.

One thing that I know,

People *are* stars,

Built by every collision,

Built by all of our scars.

LETTER TO ME

Don't wish to grow up,

Don't wish that time moved faster.

Soak it all in,

Every single second.

Time isn't guaranteed,

That's a guarantee.

Listen to your dad,

And be easy on your mom.

They will have your back,

When no one else does.

Overuse I love you,

And I'm sorry.

Lay off of the hate,

And stay out of the drama.

Watch your mouth,

It'll get you in trouble.

So will the girls,

Choose them wisely.

You'll meet them some day,

And she will make all the worries fade away.

Most of all…

I miss you.

I miss the freedom we used to have,

I miss the happy-go-lucky kid they used to know.

Before anxiety,

Before depression,

Before the cruelties of the world,

Determined how we would feel that day.

I know there are days,

You feel shaken deep in your soul.

Just stay the course,

Because God is in control.

Take it from me,

I'm being honest in this letter.

Don't rush your life away,

I promise it'll get better.

END THE STIGMA

I've been broken,

I've been bruised,

Not by anyone,

It was me who abused.

Myself,

Or a version of me.

The good,

Was something I couldn't see.

I was an addict,

To anything that faded me away.

I kept getting worse,

Casting further from grace, day-by-day.

I didn't have a rhyme,

Or a reason to be here.

Until I opened up,

And realized I had nothing to fear.

When I talked about my problems,

I felt that I had power.

Opening up,

Led me out of my darkest hour.

Men can be hurt,

And men can be depressed.

And all of that pain,

Needs to be expressed.

I'm here to end the stigma,

That men are weak,

If they talk about their problems,

Or go to therapy each week.

Men need help, too,

And that's okay.

And if you're in need of it,

Please don't hide away.

Talking is strength,

Holding it in is not.

Help me end the stigma,

And help yourself.

Made in the USA
Coppell, TX
15 November 2024